I
See
A
Miracle

Written and Illustrated
by
Lori Chown

Table of Contents

Always Believe
in
Miracles!

Lori Chown

To help you find them
I wrote this book.

I see a rainbow
after the storm.

Beautiful colors
in the sky form.

I see a miracle.

In a bird's nest
an egg is laid.

From the egg
a baby bird
is made.

I see a miracle.

I see a flower
that comes
from a seed.

Water and sun are all that it needs.

I see a miracle.

From the cocoon comes the butterfly.

The caterpillar
now has wings and
is able to fly.

I see a miracle.

Changing
from a tadpole
into a frog.

From swimming
in water to
sitting on a log.

I see a miracle.

How about you?

I see all of the creatures that live in the sea.

Breathing under water, how can it be?

I see a miracle.

How about you?

Eight round balls circling the sun.

When it comes
to life,
Earth is the
only one.

I see a miracle.

How about you?

Ten little fingers,
ten little toes.

Two ears, two eyes, and a nose.

I see a miracle.

Miracles are gifts
from the
heavens above.

So each time you
see one,
remember God's love.

About Utopian Dreams

We hope you enjoyed Utopian Dreams'
"I See A Miracle".
Please take a moment to review
this book on Amazon.com
"I See A Miracle"
Utopian Dreams' inspirational picture books are
designed to help you and your child find a little more
Faith, Hope, and Inspiration.

Learn more about Utopian Dreams at:

http://utopiandreamsgifts.webs.com

https://www.etsy.com/shop/UtopianDreamsGifts

https://www.facebook.com/Utopiandreamsgifts

http://www.amazon.com/Lori-Chown/

Coming Soon

Watch for more books from
Lori Chown, including
"A Unicorn's Wish",
Coming summer of 2016.
Utopian Dream's picture books are created to

help families share their Faith in God.

Made in the USA
Charleston, SC
28 November 2016